CHILDREN'S ENCYCLOPEDIA

THE WORLD OF KNOWLEDGE

GK

GENERAL KNOWLEDGE

Manasvi Vohra

V&S PUBLISHERS

Published by:

V&S PUBLISHERS

F-2/16, Ansari road, Daryaganj, New Delhi-110002
☎ 23240026, 23240027 • *Fax:* 011-23240028
Email: info@vspublishers.com • *Website:* www.vspublishers.com

Regional Office : Hyderabad
5-1-707/1, Brij Bhawan (Beside Central Bank of India Lane)
Bank Street, Koti, Hyderabad - 500 095
☎ 040-24737290
E-mail: vspublishershyd@gmail.com

Branch Office : Mumbai
Jaywant Industrial Estate, 1st Floor–108, Tardeo Road
Opposite Sobo Central Mall, Mumbai – 400 034
☎ 022-23510736
E-mail: vspublishersmum@gmail.com

Follow us on: t f in

DISCLAIMER

PUBLISHER'S NOTE

V&S Publishers is glad to announce the launch of a unique, set of 12 books under the head, *Children's Encyclopedia – The World of Knowledge.* The set of 12 books namely – *Physices, Chemistry, Space Science, General Sceince, Life Science, Human Body, Electronics & Communications, Scientists, Inventions & Discoveries, Transportation, The Earth, and GK (General Knowledge)* has been especially developed keeping in mind the students and children of all age groups, particularly from 6 to 14 years of age. Our main aim is to arouse the interest and solve the queries of the school children regarding the various and diverse topics of Science and help them master the subject thoroughly.

In the book, *?? - General Knowledge* focusses mainly on the amazing and interesting facts of the 'World', such as: *The Stone Age, The Story behind the Name, 'America', How was the United Kingdom formed, What is Red Cross, The Story behind Mona Lisa* and so on...

Each chapter is followed by a section called **Quick Facts** that contains a set of interesting and fascinating facts about the topics already discussed in the chapter. At the end of the book a **Glossary** of difficult words and scientific terms is given to make the book complete and comprehensive.

Quick Facts

- ❦ **When there are no more animals of a particular species left alive, that species is said to be extinct.**

Though our aim is to be flawless, but errors might have crept in inadvertently. So we request our esteemed readers to read the book thoroughly and offer valuable suggestions wherever necessary to improve and enhance the quality of the book. Hope it interests you all and serves its purpose well.

CONTENTS

The World

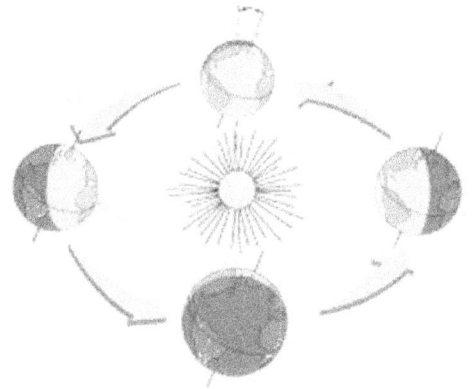

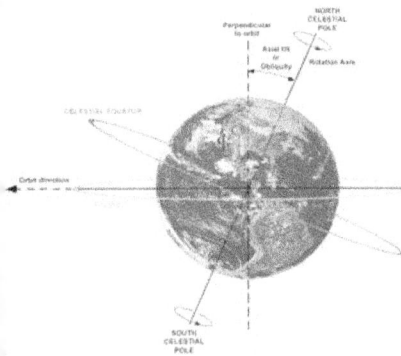

THE WORLD

Chapter - 1

THE STONE AGE

The Stone Age is that era in the history of mankind which is considered the landmark when human beings learnt to make use of **stone tools**. This age began more than three million years ago and lasted till around 5,000 years back. This age was followed by the **Bronze Age**. After this came the **Metal Age**, the time when man started using metals.

An Early Man

The Stone Age has broadly been classified into three periods:

- The Paleolithic or the Old Stone Age
- The Mesolithic or the Middle Stone Age
- The Neolithic or the New Stone Age

Old Stone Tools

The Old or the Paleolithic Stone Age is marked with the appearance of the first 'hominids' or man-like forms, for example, the Australopithecines. Men of this age were all hunters. They designed crude tools, made out of flaking stones. These tools date back to around 25,00,000 years ago. It is believed

that apart from stones, woods and bones were also made use of to fabricate tools. The Pleistoce Epoch began 25,00,000 years back and lasted till 10,000 years back. It was during the latter part of this age that 'hominids' learnt the art of making paintings on caves and also the art of sculpture.

Early Man Making Clay Pots

The Mesolithic or the Middle Stone Age began around 8000 B.C., when certain advancement started in north-western Europe. This age saw betterment in the design of the stone tools. Hunters started using tiny *flint flakes* in making harpoons and *arrows*. This age ended in 2700 B.C.

The Neolithic or the New Stone Age saw further advancement as it marked the beginning of farming and the manufacture of pottery in Europe. This age began around 9,000 years ago in the Middle East. People of this time learnt to grind and polish stones and manufactured smooth axe heads. Moreover, agriculture and domestication of animals were among the most vital characteristics of the Neolithic Age.

It was also during this time that the practice of mining had begun. Agriculture had started and people had also begun forming villages. Soon after this period, people learnt making use of metals. This marked the end of the *Stone Age* and the beginning of the *Metal Age*.

When America was discovered by the Europeans, most of the Native Americans were living in the Neolithic Stone Age. In some parts of the world, people such as the Australian aborigines and the tribes in New Guinea continued to live in the Stone Age.

- There are no written records from the Stone Age. What we know about the Stone Age humans comes from things they made, like weapons, tools, shelters and other objects discovered mostly in archaeological digs. Engraving designs on stones and bones, carved figures and drawings on the walls of caves also give us information and help us trace the slow development of Human Beings or Homo sapiens throughout the period.

- The Stone Age is divided into Paleolithic, Mesolithic and Neolithic periods, marking the progressive levels of sophistication found in artifacts and cultural activities.

- The Paleolithic Age stretches from about 2-2.5 million years BCE to 10,000 years BCE, which is about 95 percent of the time humans and their direct ancestors have been residing on this planet.

- Food was obtained mostly by hunting, fishing and collecting wild plants, nuts and fruits.

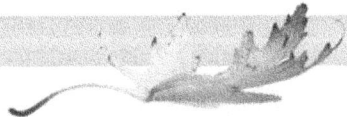

Chapter - 2

THE INTERNATIONAL DATE LINE (IDL)

It is a known fact that, with 15 degrees longitude for each hour, the Earth is divided into 24 one-hour zones. These 24 zones complete one full day on our planet. Moreover, since the Earth rotates eastward, the progression of time on the clock is westward around the world.

A Globe Showing Latitudes and Longitudes

Thus, the occurrence of 12 o'clock noon in London happens five hours before it does in Washington D.C., which is 75 degrees west of London and eight hours earlier at San Francisco, which is 120 degrees west of London. Therefore, at the time it is noon in London, it is midnight at the International Date Line or the IDL.

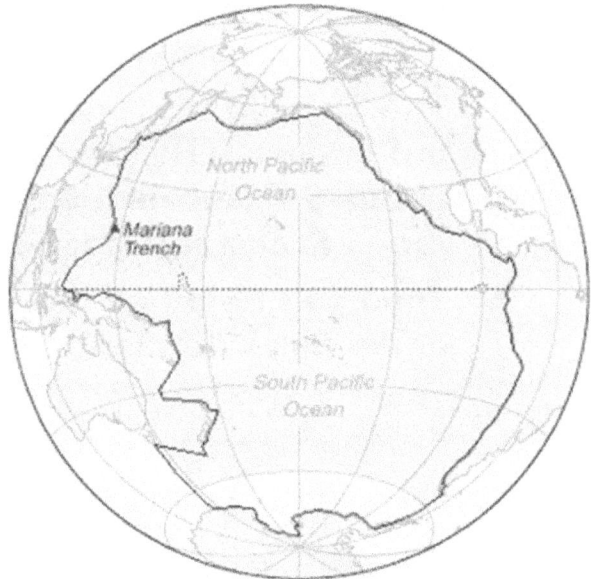

To define it in simple terms, the International Date Line can be referred to as an imaginary line, extending from the North Pole to the South Pole. On its way, it cuts through the Pacific Ocean. This line is extremely

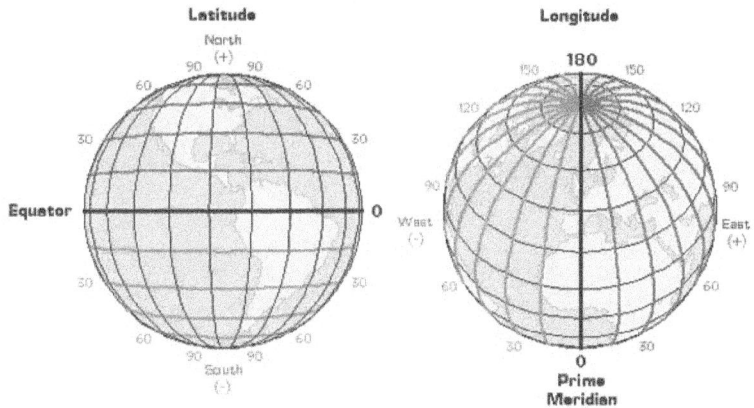

The Earth is divided into 360° Longitudes

important as it is the entire time system that the world works on. Each day on the Earth begins and ends at the International Date Line. At whichever point it crosses over land or divides nations, it gets diverted to pass over the Pacific Ocean.

This line is responsible for the deviation of east of the 180 degree Longitude to pass through the Bering Strait and include the Eastern Siberia and then towards west to include the Aleutian Islands with Alaska. Towards the south of the Equator, the line again bulges eastward to let various island groups to experience the same day as New Zealand.

What needs to be understood is that the Earth is divided into 360 longitudes vertically, 180 on both eastern and western sides. The zero degree longitude passes through Greenwich and the *180 degrees longitude is called the International Date Line*. On either sides of this line, the time is the same, but with a difference of 24 hours. It is because of this that a person who is travelling in the westward direction across the line has to adjust his calendar back by one day.

In other words, it implies that if a person crosses the International Date Line while going eastward, he gains a day, while somebody travelling in the opposite direction loses a day.

* The International Date Line (IDL) is an imaginary line that shows where the beginning of one day and the end of another come together. The Line is drawn vertically on maps and runs between the eastern tip of Russia and the western tip of Alaska, then down to the west of Hawaii, and then down to the east of New Zealand, and so on. It has several zigzags in it, too. It goes through no land except Antarctica.

* Points near the Line are almost 24 hours apart. When it is Tuesday in New Zealand, it is Monday in Hawaii. This is because the globe is divided into Time Zones that total to 24 hours. So, if you board a plane in Juneau, Alaska, on Monday and fly west to Tokyo, Japan, you will arrive on Tuesday. This is because the Earth is round.

* Many years went by before someone proposed a Date Line, opposite the Prime Meridian. It began to be drawn on maps as early as the 17th Century and was not popularly adopted until much later.

* Even today, no law proclaims that an International Date Line exists. Still, most of the globes and maps of the world include it.

Chapter - 3

THE NAME, 'AMERICA'

Today, the United States of America(USA) is the big brother of the world. Regarded as a superpower, America is one of the most powerful countries in the world. It has developed mainly in the past 100 years.

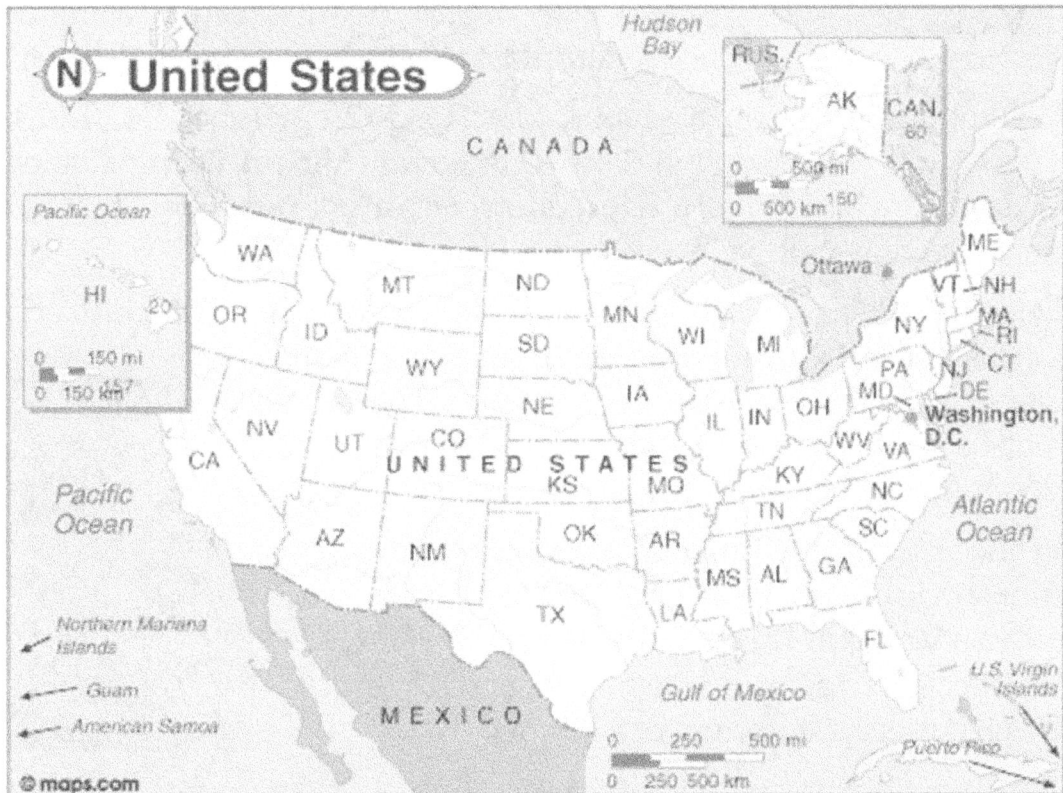

The story of the discovery of America is an interesting story. In the year 1492, the renowned Italian traveller, **Christopher Columbus** went on a sea voyage to search for India. On the morning of October 12, 1492, he arrived on an island which he named, 'San Salvador' after the King Ferdinand and Queen Isabella of Spain. Thinking it to be India, he called its inhabitants, **Indians**. This island is actually a part of America. It is presently known as the **Watling Island**.

Even though politically these people are **Native Americans** today, their descendants are often referred to as **Red Indians**. In his search for Japan, Christopher Columbus discovered **Cuba and Hispaniola**. On not being able to locate India, disappointed Columbus returned to Spain in the March of 1493.

Columbus set out on a second journey on September 24, 1493. This time he succeeded in discovering many **Virgin Islands**, such as **Jamaica** and **Puerto Rico**. However, his efforts to locate India once again went in vain.

During his third voyage in 1498, Columbus located **Trinidad** and touched upon **South America**. Around this time, a Florentine sailor called **Amerigo Vespucci** declared that he was the one to discover the mainland of South America on June 16, 1497.

In the year 1499, Amerigo Vespucci, along with Alonso de Ojeda sailed to Orinoco Straits and located **Venezuela**. Later, in the year, 1501-1502, Vespucci directed a voyage himself and discovered **Brazil** under the Portuguese banner.

Soon, it became clear to Vespucci that what Christopher Columbus had discovered as India, was not a part of Asia but a different continent altogether. Vespucci started writing about this and these were widely spread during the beginning of 1500. He went on to become the first European to discover South America.

A German geographer named **Waldsee Miller**, to honour Amerigo Vespucci, named the territory of Brazil as South America. Today, the **North America** and **South America** are collectively referred to as the *Americas*.

Quick Facts

- The United States of America (USA) is one of the largest countries in the world based on both population and land area. It has a relatively short history compared to other world nations, has one of the world's largest economies, and has one of the world's most diverse populations. As such, the United States is highly influential internationally.

- The United States is divided into 50 states. However, each state varies in size considerably. The smallest state is the Rhode Island with an area of just 1,545 square miles (4,002 sq km). By contrast, the largest state by area is Alaska with 663,268 square miles (1,717,854 sq km).

- Alaska has the longest coastline in the United States at about 6,640 miles (10,686 km).

- The Bristlecone pine trees, believed to be some of the world's oldest living things, are found in the western United States in California, Utah, Nevada, Colorado, New Mexico and Arizona. The oldest of these trees is in California and the oldest living tree itself is found in Sweden.

Chapter - 4

HOW WAS THE UK FORMED?

The United Kingdom comnprisessists of four main places which are **England, Wales, Scotland**, and **Northern Ireland**. It was formed in the year, 1801 when the 'Act of Union' enveloped Ireland under the same parliament as Scotland, Wales, and England.

The **Act of Union, 1801** described two complementary Acts, namely, the 'Union with Ireland Act 1800', an Act of the Parliament of Great Britain, and the 'Act of Union (Ireland) 1800', an Act of the Parliament of Ireland. Passed on July 2, 1800 and August 1, 1800 respectively, the twin acts united

the Kingdom of Great Britain and the Kingdom of Ireland to create the United Kingdom of Great Britain and Ireland. The union came into effect on January 1, 1801. Both acts together formed the United Kingdom, as we know it today.

In 1921, 26 Irish countries left the Union to form the *Irish Free State*, also known as the *Republic of Ireland.*

Five years later, in the year 1926, the 'Royal Parliamentary Titles Act' renamed the union. It was then called the United Kingdom of Great Britain and Northern Ireland.

The system of government followed here is that of a constitutional monarchy and the monarchy is hereditary.

Wales, being subdued by **King Edward** I in 1282, was the first to unite with **England**. Ever since Edward gave his title to his son in 1301, the heir to the English throne is called The Prince of Wales. However, it was only in 1536, when **Henry VIII**, the Tudor monarch of Welsh descent passed an Act of Union that the principle was peacefully incorporated into the kingdom.

Great Britain was introduced as the name when King James VI of Scottish origin united and succeeded the English throne as **James I** in 1603 and the two crowns. However, he could not unite the nations.

It was in the year, 1707 that another Act of Union brought Scotland and England under one government. The present flag of the United Kingdom consists of the flags of England (white with an upright red cross), the red vertical cross of Ireland, and the flag of Scotland (blue with a diagonal white cross).

The Royal Titles Act that was passed on May 29, 1953, issued the Queen the title of 'Elizabeth,, the second', by the Grace of God, of the United Kingdom of Great Britain and Northern Ireland and ofin her other realms and territories, the Queen, the Head of the Commonwealth, the Defender of the fFaith'.

Quick Facts

- The United Kingdom or UK is a developed country and has the world's seventh-largest economy by nominal Gross Domestic Product (GDP) and the eighth-largest economy by purchasing power parity. It was the world's first industrialised country and the world's foremost power during the 19th and early 20th centuries.

- UK is presently recognised as a nuclear weapons' state and its military expenditure ranks fourth in the world.

- The United Kingdom has been a permanent member of the United Nations Security Council since its first session in 1946. It has been a member of the European Union and its predecessor, the European Economic Community since 1973. It is also a member of the Commonwealth of Nations, the Council of Europe, the G7, the G8, the G20, NATO, the Organisation for Economic Cooperation and Development (OECD) and the World Trade Organisation(WTO).

Chapter - 5

THE CENSUS

The government takes a census every ten years to keep account of the population of a region. You may have noticed people coming to your house for a survey, asking about the number of family members, their age, gender, etc. This data is collected and organised. This process is called **census**.

It is known that around *4000 B.C.*, the population of the world was around *85 million*. This proves that a census was taken at that time as well. The story behind the origin of census is unknown. However, another important aspect of the census is why it is taken. The reasons behind conducting census have changed with changing scenarios of the world.

At the times of monarchies, the kings ordered for a census to assess the number of people available for wars. Another prime reason for conducting the census was for the collection of revenue. In earlier times, these were the two main reasons. However, over time, man has discovered many more uses of this process.

In today's times, one of the most important advantages of conducting a census is that it presents a clear picture of the demographics of the region it is conducted in. Aspects, such as health, education, income group, etc., can help the government in devising appropriate social schemes for the benefits of the society.

Apart from this, a census also helps in judging the increase or decrease in the population of the region. Moreover, the birth rate can be determined and a ratio between rural and urban population can be calculated.

Due to these reasons, conducting a census becomes important for a country as it helps the government of a nation to act according to the need of the hour. A population count helps a nation determine if its provisions are adequate enough. Having an approximate idea of birth rate can help a nation prepare better for its future citizens. Lastly, the study of these demographics helps in elections as it is the population that decideds the number of voters in a particular constituency.

Apart from these direct implications, a census is very useful for the betterment of law and order and other socio-economic situations.

India conducted its first census in the year 1872. Since then, it is done

every ten years. The latest census of 2012 shows the population of India to be around 1.22 billion.

Chapter - 6

THE FORMATION OF GRAND CANYON

Located in Arizona, U.S.A., the Grand Canyon is a **natural wonder of the world**. It is renowned for its spectacular view, the colourful rocks, and the majestic ambience. While travelling the Grand Canyon, one may imagine being lost in a city of rocks, with towers temples and castles in vibrant colours.

However, this panorama has a great history behind it. Have you ever wondered how The Grand Canyon was built? Well, here's your answer.

The formation of the Grand Canyon is a result of the continuous erosion of the Colorado River Valley. The immense force of the Colorado River cut out a great gorge thousands of years ago. Even now, each year the mighty force of the rushing water of this river continues to cut the bottom of this gorge deeper and deeper. This has made this the *deepest gorge in the world*.

Stretched up to 347.2 kilometers in length, the Grand Canyon is approximately 20 kilometers wide and up to 2 kilometers deep at certain places.

Since long ago, the Colorado River has been slowly cutting through the plateaus of northern Arizona, unleashing the strata of the Earth that is millions of years old. A subject of prime interest for geologists, these strata offer knowledge about the Earth's history.

An ancient *Precambrian rock* can be found at the bottom of the Canyon, where the Colorado River flows. It contains the fossils of primitive algae. In the higher strata, fossils of dinosaurs, elephants, trees, and other organisms can also be found. The top of the Canyon represents the most recent rocks. The fossils contained in the Canyon are extremely important as they provide useful insights into the evolutionary processes of the Earth's inhabitants.

The Grand Canyon is a top favourite for tourists. This spectacular site attracts more than two million tourists, each year. The Canyon offers its tourists a breathtaking view and a lot of mood swings that change just as the colour of the rocks.

In the year, 1919, the United States Government built the **Grand Canyon National Park** to promote and preserve the richness of plant and animal life that has become an integral part of this unique environment.

Quick Facts

- The geology of the Grand Canyon area exposes one of the most complete and studied sequences of rock on the Earth. The nearly 40 major sedimentary rock layers exposed in the Grand Canyon and in the Grand Canyon National Park area range in age from about 200 million to nearly 2 billion years old. Most were deposited in warm, shallow seas and sea shores in western North America. Both marine and terrestrial sediments are represented, including fossilised sand dunes from an extinct desert. There are at least 14 known unconformities in the geological record found in the Grand Canyon area.

- Wetter climates brought upon by ice ages starting 2 million years ago greatly increased the excavation of the Grand Canyon, which was nearly as deep as it is now by 1.2 million years ago. Volcanic activity deposited lava over the area 1.8 million to 500,000 years ago. At least 13 lava dams blocked the Colorado River, forming lakes that were up to 2,000 feet (610 m) deep. The end of the last ice age and subsequent human activity has greatly reduced the ability of the Colorado River to excavate the canyon.

- However, in December 2012, a study published in the journal, *Science* claimed that new tests suggested that the Grand Canyon could be as old as *70 million years*.

Chapter - 7

THE STORY BEHIND MONA LISA

The painting of **Mona Lisa** is one of the most renowned pieces of art mankind has ever witnessed. Painted by Leonardo da Vinci, it is the portrait of a woman with a mysterious smile. The painting has left people wondering what she is smiling at. Today, the *Mona Lisa painting hangs in Paris at the Louvre Museum*, which preserves the world's finest art works and antiques.

This painting was made by **Leonardo da Vinci** between 1503 and 1506. The lady in the painting, Mona Lisa, was the wife of a Florentine gentleman, Francesco del Gioconda. She was 24 at the time, the 51-year-old Leonardo started working on this painting. Mona Lisa used to come to his studio every day in the late afternoon, at the time the light was soft.

This painting was worked on for four years, during which Leonardo da Vinci became fascinated with both his model and the portrait. That is why this portrait has retained an exclusive ambience around itself.

Mona Lisa's face, charismatic and graceful, has amazed billions of people over the years. It seems like the painting has life in it. The background is mysteriously portrayed as a misty scenery.

It is known that Leonardo da Vinci was so obsessed with the painting himself that he never gave it to Francesco. He always made an excuse and carried it with him wherever he went. It is also believed that while he was working on the painting, he used jesters, musicians, etc. to keep his model in a merry mood.

When Leonardo came to France in 1516, **King Francis** gave him a beautiful mansion in the Loire valley. He offered him 4,000 gold crowns for the painting but could not acquire it till Leonardo's death in 1519. Since then, the painting has been a possession of the emperors of France.

It is remarkable that in the past 450 years, the painting has gone out of France only twice. In 1911, the painting was stolen, but found two years later in Italy. The second time, the painting went missing for 26 days, while it was taken during an amazingly well-guarded and immensely insured visit to the United States of America as a guest of the then **President, John F. Kennedy**.

- Leonardo used a pyramid design to place the woman simply and calmly in the space of the painting. Her folded hands form the front corner of the pyramid. Her breast, neck and face glow in the same light that models her hands. The light gives the variety of living surfaces an underlying geometry of spheres and circles. Leonardo referred to a seemingly simple formula for the seated female figure: the images of seated Madonna, which were widespread at the time. He effectively modified this formula in order to create the visual impression of distance between the sitter and the observer. The armrest of the chair functions as a dividing element between Mona Lisa and the viewer.

- The woman sits markedly upright with her arms folded, which is also a sign of her reserved posture. Only her gaze is fixed on the observer and seems to welcome him to this silent communication. Since the brightly lit face is practically framed with various much darker elements (hair, veil, shadows), the observer's attraction to it is brought to even greater extent. The woman appears alive to an unusual measure, which Leonardo achieved by his new method by not drawing the outlines.

- Some art historians of the Eastern art, such as *Yukio Yashiro*, also argue that the landscape in the background of the picture was influenced by the *Chinese paintings*.

Chapter - 8

WHAT IS RED CROSS?

An international humanitarian organisation, called the **Red Cross Foundation** is devoted to alleviate all kinds of human suffering. The Red Cross has offices in almost all countries of the world that help people regardless of their sex, race, colour, etc. at times of both *peace and war*.

The Red Cross Flag

In times of peace, its goals are to provide first aid, provide safe drinking water, prevent accidents, train nurses, set up hospitals, establishing blood banks, etc. On the other hand, at times of war, its main objective is to provide healthcare to wounded soldiers and victims.

Henri Dunant

The origin of this organisation is very engaging. The founder of Red Cross, **Henri Dunant**, a *Swiss banker* had gone to the city of **Lombardy in Italy** for business in 1859. The city at that time was the focus of the 'Battle of Solferino', between Australia and France.

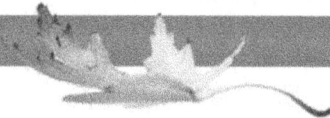

Dunant witnessed thousands of wounded people, desperate for help, lying all around the roads. He was overwhelmed by the sight and regardless of his work, started setting up local healthcare centres in association with the villagers. He saved many lives through his actions.

Three years after the war, Dunant wrote a book called, 'A Memory of Solferino', appealing to the people of the world to form relief societies for people affected by war. His idea gained worldwide recognition and in the International Conference of 1864 held in **Geneva**, **16 countries** agreed to set up the **Red Cross Societies**.

Thus, the Red Cross came into existence. It came to be known as the organisation whose motive is to relieve people from their sufferings caused by any kind of calamity.

The Red Cross has three organs. First is the *International Committee* which consists of *25 citizens of Switzerland*. Its main office is in Geneva. The second is the *League of the Red Cross Foundation* and the third is the *National Red Cross Society*.

At times of war, the International Committee looks after the prisoners of war and arranges for their proper healthcare. It also helps them connect to their relatives.

It also serves the people affected by natural disasters, such as, cyclones, tsunamis, etc. The Red Cross Organisation, in another word, is a *friend to humanity*.

- The International Red Cross and Red Crescent Movement, born of a desire to bring assistance without discrimination to the wounded on the battlefield endeavours, in its international and national capacity, to prevent and alleviate human suffering wherever it may be found. Its purpose is to protect life and health and to ensure respect for the human beings. It promotes mutual understanding, friendship, cooperation and lasting peace among all the people.

- It makes no discrimination as to nationality, race, religious beliefs, class or political opinions. It endeavours to relieve the suffering of individuals, being guided solely by their needs, and to give priority to the most urgent cases of distress.

- It is a voluntary relief movement not prompted in any manner by desire for gain.

- There can be only one the Red Cross or one Red Crescent Society in any one country. It must be open to all. It must carry on its humanitarian work throughout its territory.

- The International Red Cross and the Red Crescent Movement, in which all Societies have equal status and share equal responsibilities and duties in helping each other, is worldwide.

Chapter - 9

THE SEVEN WONDERS OF THE ANCIENT WORLD

The world's most exquisite and wonderful architectural creations are referred to as the *Wonders of the World*. These wonders can be broadly classified into two categories - the *seven wonders of the ancient world* and the seven wonders *of the modern world*.

The wonders of the ancient world were regarded as magnificent creations of early civilisations by the Romans and the Greeks. The ancient seven wonders of the world consist of the following:

- *The Pyramids of Egypt*
- *The Hanging Gardens of Babylon*
- *The Tomb of Mausolus*
- *The Temple of Artemis (Diana)*
- *The Colossus of Rhodes of Helios*
- *The Statue of Zeus*
- *The Light House of Pharos near Alexandria*

The Pyramids of Egypt: The Great Pyramid of Giza (also known as the Pyramid of Khufu or the Pyramid of Cheops) is the oldest and largest of the three pyramids in the **Giza Necropolis** bordering what is now **El Giza, Egypt**. It is the oldest of the Seven Wonders of the Ancient World, and the only one to remain largely intact. Egyptologists believe that the pyramid was built as a tomb for the fourth dynasty Egyptian Pharaoh Khufu (Cheops in Greek) over a 10 to 20-year period concluding around 2560 BCE. Initially at, 146.5 metres (481 feet), the Great Pyramid was the tallest man-made structure in the world for over 3,800 years. Originally, the **Great Pyramid** was covered by casing stones that formed a smooth outer surface; what is seen today is the underlying core structure. Some of the casing stones that once covered the structure can still be seen around the base. There have been varying scientific and alternative theories about the Great Pyramid's construction techniques. Most accepted construction hypotheses are based on the idea that it was built by moving huge stones from a quarry and dragging and lifting them into place.

There are **three known chambers** inside the Great Pyramid. The lowest chamber is cut into the bedrock upon which the pyramid was built and was unfinished. The so-called Queen's Chamber and the King's Chamber are higher up within the pyramid structure. The **The Great Pyramid of Giza** is the only pyramid in Egypt known to contain both ascending and descending passages. The main part of the Giza complex is a setting of buildings that included two mortuary temples in the honour of Khufu (one close to the pyramid and one near the Nile), three smaller pyramids for Khufu's wives, an even smaller 'satellite' pyramid, a raised causeway connecting the two temples, and small mastaba tombs surrounding the pyramid for the nobles.

The Hanging Gardens of Babylon: These were one of the Seven Wonders of the Ancient World, and the only one of the wonders that may have been purely legendary. They were purposely built in the ancient city-state of Babylon, near present-day Al Hillah, Babil province, in Iraq. The Hanging Gardens were not the only World Wonder in Babylon; the city walls and obelisk attributed to Queen Semiramis were also featured in the ancient list of Wonders. The gardens were attributed to the Neo-Babylonian king Nebuchadnezzar II, who ruled between 605 and 562 BC. He is reported to have constructed the gardens to please his homesick wife Amytis of Media, who longed for the plants of her homeland. The gardens were said to have been destroyed by several earthquakes after the 2nd century BC. The Hanging Gardens of Babylon are documented by ancient Greek and Roman writers, including Strabo, Diodorus Siculus, and Quintus Curtius Rufus. However, no cuneiform texts describing the Hanging Gardens are extant, and no definitive archaeological evidence concerning their whereabouts have been found.

The Tomb of Mausolus: One of the Seven Wonders of the Ancient World, the mausoleum was the tomb of Mausolus, from where the name came, and it was the most enduring achievement of his wife and sister Artemisia, the Younger,

who, after Mausolu's death in 352 BC, had it built in his honour. Mausolu's tomb became one of the most famous architectural showpieces of antiquity; it was named one of the *Seven Wonders of the World by the travel writers* of the *Hellenistic era*. It consisted of a solid rectangular base topped by 36 Ionic columns. These were surmounted by a pyramid and crowned with a massive statue of Mausolus and Artemisia riding a chariot, reaching a total height of 60 metres. The base was adorned with a frieze executed by four of the leading sculptors of ancient Greece, one per side; classical writers were most impressed by these sculptures.

For at least the last 20 years, a Danish team of archaeologists and conservators, led by Prof. Kristian Jeppesen of the Aarhus University in Denmark, has been excavating and preserving the little remains of the site, consisting on the funerary underground chamber and architectural remains, many of them were found in the vicinity and the castle. The Mausoleum Museum was opened in 1988, thanks to the joint auspices of the Turkish and Danish governments, now under the management of the *Bodrum Museum of Underwater Archaeology*.

The Temple of Artemis: Also known less precisely as the *Temple of Diana*, was a Greek temple dedicated to a **goddess,** Greeks identified as **Artemis** and was one of the Seven Wonders of the Ancient World. It was located in Ephesus (near the modern town of Selçuk in present-day

Turkey), and was completely rebuilt three times before its eventual destruction in 401. Only foundations and sculptural fragments of the latest of the temples at the site remain.

The Colossus of Rhodes: This was a statue of the *Greek Titan Helios*, erected in the city of Rhodes on the *Greek island of Rhodes* by *Chares of Lindos* between 292 and 280 BC. It is considered one of the Seven Wonders of the Ancient World. It was constructed to celebrate Rhodes' victory over the ruler of Cyprus, Antigonus I Monophthalmus, whose son unsuccessfully besieged Rhodes in 305 BC. Before its destruction in the earthquake of 226 BC, the Colossus of Rhodes stood over 30 metres (107 ft) high, making it one of the tallest statues of the ancient world.

The Statue of Zeus: This statue was located on the west coast of *Greece at Olympia*. In the antiquity, this city was a place of cult which contained numerous treasures of the Greek art: temples, monuments, altars, theaters, statues and marble or bronze votive offerings. It was realised with golden and ivory, measured 12 m (39 feet) height and was placed on a base of 2 m (7 feet). The base of the statue was 6 m (21 feet) wide and 1 m height. The statue's perimeter was 13 m (43 feet). This work touched almost the ceiling of the temple. On the other hand, the throne was decorated with precious stones, ivory, ebony and gold.

Zeus, in the sitting position, holds, in its right hand, the goddess of Victory, Nike, and, in the left hand, a scepter surmounted by an eagle. The throne was decorated with relief sculptured mythological scenes, notably evoking the murder of the sons of Niobe, the Queen of Thebes.

The Light House of Pharos near Alexandria: The Lighthouse was built on the Island of Pharos in the harbour of Alexandria, Egypt. It was built around 290 BCE. It was a working lighthouse that helped ships find their way safely into the harbour. It was also a tourist attraction. Visitors could buy food at the observation platform on the first level. Anyone who wished to could climb nearly to the top. There were not many places in the ancient world that visitors could climb a man-made structure, 300 feet up, to view the sea.

The Lighthouse stood for over 1500 years. Scientists believe an earthquake topped the Lighthouse during the 1300's. Divers today search for remains at the bottom of the Mediterranean Sea. It was situated in Egypt, near Alexandria. Made out of white marble, it was constructed in 279 B.C. and was 122 metres high. It remained till 796 A.D. of these, only *The Pyramids of Egypt are intact today.*

- The construction of these wonders is an interesting story. The surviving Pyramids of Egypt were built around 5,000 years back. They were the tombs of the ancient Pharos or Kings. The biggest Pyramid is located near Cairo, in a town called Giza. This was the tomb of Pharaoh Cheops and his queen.

- Spread across an area of 5 hectares, its base forms a square and is approximately 147 meters high. The construction of thise tomb of Pharaoh Cheops took over one lakh labourers and about 20 years.

- The Hanging Gardens of Babylon were built in the 9th century B.C. by King Nebuchadnezzar for his wife Amytis. Built with a series of terraces, one on top of the other, they were 7.6 metre thick and trees grew on each terrace. Irrigation in these high gardens was done through pumping water from river Euphrates. After the Persians took control of the place, people left as it was in ruins.

- The third wonder, The Tomb of Mausolus was built by the ruler of Halicarnassus, King Marsolus. Though he died before the tomb was completed, his wife Artemesia looked into its construction. It was 42.6 meters high with a statue of the king and queen riding a horse chariot. It eventually collapsed but its remains are preserved in the British Museum, London.

- The Temple of Artemis (Diana) of Ephesus with its roof rested on two rows of approximately 200 metres high, was constructed in the honour of the Goddess in 550 B.C. A mad man burnt it down in 365 B.C. Alexander the Great rebuilt it in 250 B.C.

Glossary

Aberration: A deviation from the proper or expected course; abnormal

Contentious: Something that can be argued

Diurnal Birds: Birds which see better in the day than at night

Fermentation: The process of conversion of sugars into ethanol; fermentation of milk leads to the preparation of curd, etc.

Galactic: Within a galaxy

Homogenised: The process of reducing fat from milk

Nocturnal Birds: Birds which see better during the night than in day time

Poaching: Illegal hunting

Predicament: A problem

Renowned: Well known

Rods and cones: Special cells which help in the clarity of vision

Pyramind: A massive monument of ancient Egypt with rectangular base and four triangular faces

Lighthouse: A tall structure tapped by a powerful light as signal to help boats and ships

Harbour: A sheltered port for anchoring a ship

Obsessed: Preoccupied; inclined excessively

Immensely: Extremely large; tremendously

www.ingramcontent.com/pod-product-compliance
Lightning Source LLC
LaVergne TN
LVHW061221060426
835508LV00014B/1395